# HOW TO BE MADE WHOLE

# HOW TO BE MADE WHOLE

Apostle Dr. Burley Knowles

| Library of Congress Control Number: | | 2016902245 |
|---|---|---|
| ISBN: | Hardcover | 978-1-5144-5953-9 |
| | Softcover | 978-1-5144-5954-6 |
| | eBook | 978-1-5144-5955-3 |

Scripture quotations marked NKJV are taken from the New King James Version. Copyright © 1982 by Thomas Nelson, Inc. Used by permission. All rights reserved.

Scripture quotations marked MSG are taken from THE MESSAGE. Copyright © 1993, 1994, 1995, 1996, 2000, 2001, 2002, 2003 by Eugene H. Peterson. Used by permission of NavPress Publishing Group. Website.

Scriptures marked as CEV are taken from the *Contemporary English Version* Copyright © 1995 by American Bible Society. Used by permission.

Scripture quotations marked NIV are taken from the *Holy Bible, New International Version®*. NIV®. Copyright © 1973, 1978, 1984 by International Bible Society. Used by permission of Zondervan. All rights reserved. [Biblica]

Scripture quotations marked KJV are from the Holy Bible, King James Version (Authorized Version). First published in 1611. Quoted from the KJV Classic Reference Bible, Copyright © 1983 by the Zondervan Corporation.

Scripture quotations marked AMP are from *The Amplified Bible*, Old Testament copyright © 1965, 1987 by the Zondervan Corporation. *The Amplified Bible*, New Testament copyright © 1954, 1958, 1987 by the Lockman Foundation. Used by permission. All rights reserved.

Any people depicted in stock imagery provided by Thinkstock are models, and such images are being used for illustrative purposes only. Certain stock imagery © Thinkstock.

Print information available on the last page.

Rev. date: 04/26/2016

**To order additional copies of this book, contact:**
Xlibris
1-888-795-4274
www.Xlibris.com
Orders@Xlibris.com
707055

# Contents

# Introduction

It is time for us, the body of Christ, to unlock our full potential and become all that we can be; however, there are many of us in the body of Christ who have been wounded, offended, abused, and cast aside. There are many who started out in the faith but, somehow, someway, fell prey to the snares of the enemy (Satan) and, as a result, have become ineffective members of the body. These attacks are orchestrated to distract us from our purpose. As a result, there are many Christians who simply find it difficult to align (yield) their spirit, soul, and body to God's Word.

Over the years, I've realized that there are so many who have been victimized, and it seems that they are unable to recover; although our physical bodies can and, in most cases, does heal itself, there are those who still find it difficult to go on because they must undergo a healing of the soul (which consists of the mind, the will, and the emotions) and spirit (which is also referred to as the heart). Jesus asked a paralyzed man, "Will you be made whole?" (John 5:6) It is God's will for us to be whole (complete), at peace, and have solace in our spirit, soul, and body.

The Bible declares in Hosea 4:6, "My people are destroyed for a lack of knowledge. Because you have rejected knowledge, I also will reject you from being my priest for Me; because you have forgotten the law of your God, I also will forget your children." There is one major point in this passage. The point of this passage is that God's people are destroyed for a lack of knowledge not because they were not privy to it but that they have rejected the knowledge of his Word. This places some in one of two categories: either they lacked the knowledge of the Word of God through anemic teaching, or they just outright rejected the knowledge of God's Word, his Spirit, and his presence. It is either the lack or the rejection of knowledge that Satan will exploit: the lack of knowing or the rejecting of how fearfully and wonderfully we are made; the lack of knowing or the rejecting that we are complete in him; the lack of knowing or rejecting of how to align or submit our spirit, soul, and body with the Word of God; and also not knowing or refusing the purpose God has for our lives. This has allowed the enemy to cripple and, in some cases, destroy many in the body of Christ and their families as well.

By utilizing the Word, faith, God's Spirit (Holy Spirit), and God's presence, we will strengthen, edify, or build up and establish ourselves as we come to the realization that we are not mere flesh and blood but we are supernatural spirit beings. We will gain a greater revelation of the God who created us in his image and likeness. This will provoke us to establish a deeper, spiritually grounded relationship with God the Father, a newfound adoration for his Son, Jesus Christ, thus causing us to establish a deeper fellowship with his Spirit. This will allow us to understand that we are complete in him, thus causing us to discover what his will is for our lives and, as a result, give our lives purpose and meaning. This will motivate us to position ourselves in God's kingdom and once again become effective and fruitful members in the body.

It is my prayer that this book will eradicate any pressing and opposing problems you may have encountered and that you become the person the Father has predestined and purposed you to be and complete his will for your life. God bless.

# Chapter 1

## To Be Whole or Not to Be Whole

To be whole or not to be whole, that is definitely the question. What does it mean to be whole? The *Webster's Dictionary* defines *whole* as "complete; having nothing missing." The *Webster's Thesaurus* uses such words as *total, sound, hale, unimpaired, entire, intact,* and *perfect* to describe the word *whole*. The Greek word for the word *whole*, which is the same word for the word *entire*, is *tolokleros*, which means "complete, sound in every part." The Hebrew word *shalom* (which means "peace") is derived from a root word meaning "wholeness," complete in every area and facet of our lives, so there is peace in being whole. The *Strong's Concordance* gives 259 references of the word *whole*. With all this talk about being whole, you would think it is of some importance; you bet it is!

God the Father, Jesus the Son, and the Holy Spirit all created us (mankind) in his image and his likeness. Genesis 1:1 says,

> In the beginning God created the heavens and the earth.

The Hebrew word for God in this text is Elohim, which is the plural name of God, referring to all three. We were literally created to look like them and do what they do. Genesis 1:26–28 (MSG) reads,

> God spoke: "Let Us make human beings in our image, make them reflecting our nature so that they can be responsible for the fish of the sea, the birds of the air, the cattle, and, yes, earth itself, and every animal that moves on the face of the earth." God created human beings; He created them godlike, reflecting God's nature. He created them male and female. God blessed them: "Prosper! Reproduce! Fill the earth! Take charge! Be responsible for the fish in the sea and birds in the air, for every living thing that moves on the face of the earth."

God the Father, Jesus the Son, and the Holy Spirit came together and collaborated on creating us and granted us certain qualities and abilities to glorify him in the earth. The phrase "image and likeness" simply means to resemble him and do what he does. Our Heavenly Father reigns, rules, and dominates. There is no one greater, and that power was handed down, but it certainly is no hand-me-down! We can use that power to keep the devil at bay and defeat him in every way.

He has temporarily given this dominion and authority to his Son, Jesus, until all things are under his feet. It reads in 1 Corinthians 15:24–28 (NKJV),

> Then comes the end, when He delivers the kingdom to God the Father, when He puts an end to all rule and all authority and power. For He must reign till He has put all enemies under His feet. The last enemy that will be destroyed is death. For "He has put all things under His feet." But when He says "all things are put under Him," It is evident that He who put all things under Him is excepted. Now when all things are made subject to Him, then the Son Himself will also be subject to Him who put all things under Him that God may be all in all.

Jesus then deputized us with the same authority to exercise the same dominion that he did over Satan and his evil minions. Yes, the same authority to exercise dominion in the earth over all satanic forces and oppositions. Let's take a look at what Jesus said in the Gospel of John:

> The person who trusts Me will not only do what I'm doing but even greater things, because I, on my way to the Father, am giving you the same work to do that I've been doing. You can count on it. John 14:12 (MSG)

We have been given both the authority of the Word of God and the blessed gift of having his Spirit placed in every believer. Jesus literally franchised himself by sending the Holy Spirit to reside in everyone who believes in him and receives the Holy Spirit. We can now become Spirit-filled believers, enabling us to do what he did on the earth. He has granted us the authority that the Father intended for us to have in the beginning. Now Jesus is sitting at the right hand of the Father, interceding for us. What exactly do you think Jesus is interceding for? I believe Jesus is interceding that the power of God's Word be revealed to us, and we begin through faith to transform the logos (or the written Word) into the *rhema* (or spirit-life Word). How do we do this? We do it by exercising our faith and working the Word of God and utilizing the authority given us, thereby allowing his glory to be revealed in us. The Bible says that the Word of God is quick (life giving), powerful, sharper than a double-edged sword (Hebrews 4:12). The Word of God mingled with faith is a powerful weapon against Satan and his dark forces. We have been given the authority to drive the devil out of every facet of our lives, out of our bodies, our families, and our finances and anyone else's life. You are an overcomer! The Bible says,

> For whatever is born of God overcomes the world.
> And this is the victory that has overcome the
> world—our faith. 1 John 5:4 (NKJV)

Why? Well, because our great and awesome God has placed his Spirit in us. Jesus said,

"The words that I speak to you they are spirit, and
they are life. John 6:63 (NKJV)

We need to hear the Word, receive the Word, love the Word,
and most importantly, do the Word. We must first hear the Word
because faith comes by hearing and not just hearing anything but
hearing the Word of God (Romans 10:17).

Faith is the transforming agent that causes the written Word
to become a spirit-life Word that if spoken in faith, now becomes
the Word that is quick (or life giving), sharper than any double-
edged sword. We must learn to live by faith and trust in the power
of God's Word.

But without faith no one can please God. We must
believe He is real and that He rewards everyone
who searches for Him. Hebrews 11:6 (CEV)

The Bible declares that the Word pierces and divides, or
separates, the soul from the spirit. We are fearfully and wonderfully
made by God. Each part of the Trinity is represented in man. God
is a spirit; his persona is revealed through the Holy Spirit, and
his body is our Lord and Savior, Jesus Christ. In Genesis 1:26,
God the Father suggested to the Son and the Holy Spirit to make
mankind in their image and likeness (to resemble him and do
what he does), and he did it with the intent of man walking in
the authority that he had provided. He gave man dominion over
everything on the earth. God gave full authority to Jesus, and

every creature on the earth, above the earth, and under the earth must bow. Jesus then deputized us with the same authority that the Father had given him.

We are spirits, we have a soul, and we live in a body. It is imperative that we understand that we are so fearfully and wonderfully made by God. We have to realize that we are more of a spirit being than we are flesh. Unfortunately, it does not become a reality to most of us until we are faced with death or are dying. In the book of Psalms, King David declared the following:

> I will praise You, for I am fearfully and wonderfully made; Marvelous are your works, and that my soul knows very well. Psalm 139:14 (NKJV)

David understood the importance of knowing how special God has made us. I'm not just talking about the image we see in the mirror but the spirit (the eternal being) and the soul (the renewed and reformed component) of man as well. Our Father loves us so much that he literally made us little replicas of himself. Not almighty but strong enough to defeat the devil. In Psalm the eighth chapter King David inquires,

> Then I ask, "Why do you care about us humans? Why are you concerned for us weaklings?" You made us a little lower than you yourself, and you have crowned us with glory and honor. Psalm 8:4–5 (CEV)

The New King James Version of verse 5 reads, "You have made him [man] a little lower than the angels." This was a breakdown in translation because the original manuscript read, "You have made him [man] a little lower than Elohim [God in plural form]." Why is man so fearfully and wonderfully made? Why did he make us a little lower than himself? It's because he loves us so very much. God loves us so much that even when Adam sinned and forfeited his power and position—and not him only but all mankind—the Father sent Jesus to both redeem and restore. Jesus redeemed us by placing us back in right standing with God and restoring the dominion we were given in the beginning. It reads in 3 John 2 (CEV),

> Dear friend, and I pray that all goes well for you. I hope you are as strong in body, as I know you are in spirit.

God the Father is concerned about us and wants us to prosper in every aspect of life. He is concerned about every part of us, our spirit, soul, and body. Jesus said that the very hairs on our head are numbered by God. That's great concern. There is no greater love than that. Need I remind you that he loves us so much that he gave his Son, Jesus, for our redemption and forgiveness of sin, entitling us to eternal life. Our Heavenly Father did not place us here to fail; he placed us here to succeed. Each one of us has a predetermined purpose that God has installed well before the foundation of the world; however, we must decide to submit to that predetermined purpose. It will be far greater than anything in life we would ever endeavor to pursue.

For He chose us in Him before the creation of the world to be holy and blameless in His sight in love. Ephesians 1:4 (NIV)

For those who God foreknew he also predestined to be conformed to the image of His Son, that He may be the firstborn among many brothers and sisters. Romans 8:29 (NIV)

God predestined or predetermined for us to be conformed in the image of Jesus by following the pattern and standard that Jesus established so that those who will do so become sons and daughters of God. If any of you have older siblings, you've heard your parents ask, "Why can't you be more like your older brother?" God created, equipped, enabled, and established us to become like our big brother, Jesus. Jesus's purpose now is to intercede that we will become more like him each and every day. The Holy Spirit's main purpose is to lead you to and throughout that predestinate purpose, if you allow him. He has given us everything we need to become successful. The scripture says,

We have everything we need to live a life that pleases God. It was all given to us by God's own power, when we learned that He had invited us to share in His wonderful goodness. 2 Peter 1:3 (CEV)

He has given us all we need to live a successful, or abundant, as well as a godly life. He's even given us a purpose in life. Before we were known, the Father predestined (began and ended) a purpose for us. He indeed set us up to succeed and not to fail. We must read the Word, study it, meditate on it, confess it, and align ourselves with it in order to be whole or successful. In addition, we must also establish an open relationship with the Holy Spirit. Joshua 1:8 (NKJV) reads,

> This Book of the Law shall not depart from your mouth, but you shall meditate in it [the Word] day and night, that you may observe to do according to all that is written in it. For then [you] will make [your] way prosperous, and then [you] will have good success.

We must allow God's presence and his Word to have preeminence in our lives if we are to ever going to be successful and bear fruit, thereby giving glory to God. The very moment we decide to keep the Word of God inside and ever before us, then and only then shall we will experience good success. The Word of God is a vital part in our becoming whole. It is this good success that causes others to gravitate to God. Jesus said,

> Let your light so shine before men, that they may see your good works and glorify your Father in heaven. Matthew 5:16 (NKJV)

It is a combination of our behavior coupled with the success that results from that behavior that wins the crowd. This enables us to bear fruit (win souls) for the Lord.

> This is to My Father's glory, that you bear much fruit, showing yourselves to be my disciples. John 15:8 (NIV)

It is very important that we are whole so that we can bear fruit. This is why the devil attacks us—in order to distract us from our primary purpose, which is to win souls for the Lord and set those who are bound by the devil free. In addition, we must establish his kingdom on the earth. He (the devil) attacks our body, he attacks our finances, and he attacks our family in an effort to wound us spiritually, physically, and mentally. When we are wounded, we become counterproductive to God, ourselves, and everyone around us. We must maintain a state of wholeness to defeat the enemy and be fruitful in every area and aspect of our lives. In John 15:16 (CEV), Jesus said,

> You did not chose me, I chose you and sent you out to produce fruit, the kind of fruit that will last. Then my Father will give you whatever you ask for in my name.

Jesus said that the Father has chosen us not only to be saved but also to win others to the kingdom (bear fruit). He also wants us to disciple the fruits until they are stable and able to stand on their own (remain). This is why we are under constant attack by Satan—in order to bind and hinder us, preventing us from doing what we were created to do. This is why we must be made whole, so we can fully accomplish the great commission. The Apostle Paul wrote the following:

> I pray that the God who gives peace [shalom, wholeness] will make you completely holy and may your spirit, soul, and body be kept healthy and faultless until our Lord Jesus returns. 1 Thessalonians 5:23 (CEV)

God wants us whole more than anything in this world, for our benefit and the benefit of all we encounter in this life. Before the foundation of the world, he chose us in him. Ephesians 1:4 (CEV) reads,

> Before the world was created, God had Christ choose us to live with Him and be His holy, and innocent, and loving people.

God loves us so much that before he spoke the world in existence, he chose us in him. Even before we were created, he had already prepared a place and a purpose for us. What is that purpose, you may ask? Be fruitful and multiply. Bear fruit after your kind. Not just natural fruit but spiritual fruit. Romans 8:28–29 (CEV) reads,

We know that God is always at work for the good of everyone who loves Him. They are the ones who God has chosen for His purpose and He has always known who His chosen ones would be. He has decided to let them become like His own son so that His son would be the first of many children.

God has given us a purpose that has a happy ending. He knew us before we were known. Then he gave us a wonderful future. He was so determined to accomplish this that he sowed his Son, Jesus, in order to receive an unlimited harvest of sons. Hallelujah, that's really good news! Jeremiah writes in chapter 29 verse 11 (NKJV),

> For I know the thoughts I think toward you, says the LORD, thoughts of peace and not of evil, to give you a future and a hope.

This is our predetermined purpose. Truly, we serve an awesome God. We must stand on the Word and start receiving all that the Father has promised us, and we must believe that future, that hope, that predetermined purpose has a guaranteed happy ending.

When we exercise the God-given authority that has been restored to us by Jesus Christ, we will be successful in all we do. God wants us whole, complete, hale in our spirit, soul, and body so that we will be productive members of the body of Christ and bring others into the kingdom (bear fruit).

There is a serious decision or choice we must make. Either we trust God, walk in his Word, and be whole, or be victimized by the devil. Psalm 82:6–7 (CEV) reads,

> I, the Most High God, say that all of you are gods and also my own children. But you will die, just like everyone else, including powerful rulers.

Yes, the scripture is referring to believers as gods, meaning the judges of the Father's footstool, the earth. This was no misprint, nor was it a contradiction, because Jesus confirmed this in John 10:34 (NKJV).

> Jesus answered them, "Is it not written in your Law, 'I said, "You are gods"'?

No, we are not to be worshipped, but we are called to give glory to God and glorify him as we execute his Word and his will in the earth. We have been given the power and authority over the devil to effect change both in our lives and the life of others. It is up to us to decide whether we are to be made whole. God has already paved the way for us to live victorious, but it must become a reality to us. To be whole or not to be whole? That is the question. Will you be made whole? God is not just concerned about our spiritual well-being but our physical as well. It says in 3 John 2 (KJV),

Beloved, I wish above all things that thou mayest prosper and be in health, even as thy soul prospereth.

It is God's will for us to prosper and to be healthy as we grow more and more spiritually. It is God's will that we are whole, that we may be able to minister to those who are lost, hurting, and those who have gone astray. Let's look at another passage of scripture:

Wherefore henceforth know we no man after the flesh: yea, though we have known Christ after the flesh, yet now henceforth know we Him no more. Therefore if any man be in Christ, he is a new creature: old things are passed away; behold all things are become new. And all things are of God, who hath reconciled us to Himself by Jesus Christ, and hath given to us the ministry of reconciliation; To wit, that God was in Christ, reconciling the world unto Himself not imputing their trespasses unto them; and hath committed unto us the word of reconciliation. Now then we are ambassadors for Christ, as though God did beseech you by us: we pray you in Christ's stead, be ye reconciled to God. For He hath made him to be sin for us, who knew no sin; that we might be made the righteousness of God in Him. 2 Corinthians 5:16–21 (KJV)

God the Father looked beyond our evil deeds to see us beyond the flesh. He has called us to know everyone after the spirit. If we know others by the spirit, by the way, it prevents us from being judgmental and criticizing others, both believers and nonbelievers. We can fully understand that we as believers are all new creatures in Christ Jesus. God loved us so much that he reconciled us to himself through his Son, Jesus, and now has given us the ministry of reconciliation. Now we're responsible for sharing God's love with others. It is imperative that we are whole in our spirit, soul, and body in order to reconcile others back to our Father. We're committed to the word of reconciliation, meaning it is our lifelong goal and purpose to win others into the kingdom. Verse 20 refers to us as ambassadors for Christ. As an ambassador, it is imperative that we are reconciled to God and are able to represent him well. Like Ambassadors, they represent their country while residing in another country. They are not governed by the laws of that country but that of the country they represent. As ambassadors for Christ, we must demonstrate the authority that has been given to us from a kingdom not of this world by walking in faith and power. In 2 Corinthians 1:3-4, (NKJV), Paul writes,

> Blessed be the God and Father of our Lord Jesus Christ, the Father of mercies and God of all comfort, who comforts us in all our tribulation, that we may be able to comfort those who are in any trouble, with the comfort with which we ourselves are comforted of God.

Our Heavenly Father is there to comfort us in times of need. However, he does it with an ulterior motive, and that is that we may be able to comfort someone else with the same comfort that we've received from him. This is why the body of Christ must be made whole, that we will be able to comfort those who are hurting, because if we're still hurt, we will minister pain instead of comfort to those who are hurting. An injured person is no good to someone who's injured, and no one wants a sick physician operating on them. How much more ineffective are we if we attempt to minister to others while we're still hurting?

God has equipped us with his Holy Spirit for that very purpose. In fact, he (the Holy Spirit) is referred to as the comforter (one of many names), and his purpose in us is not merely for us to speak in tongues, dance, and shout when we are inspired to do so but to minister to others. The book of Acts explains the purpose of the Holy Spirit in our lives as described in the ministry of Jesus. Let's look at verse 38 of chapter 10 (KJV).

> How God anointed Jesus of Nazareth with the Holy Ghost and with power: who went about doing good, and healing all that were oppressed of the devil; for God was with him.

God anointed Jesus with the Holy Spirit, enabling Him to go around doing good things and healing all who were oppressed by the devil.

We all have the same Holy Spirit dwelling in us, that same Holy Spirit who brooded over the face of the earth, awaiting God's word that he could create whatever God had spoken, and he's waiting inside us to change situations and circumstances in both our lives and the lives of others, but only when we speak the Word in faith, believing. We have to believe that God is able and that he's faithful to his Word. John 14:12 (KJV) says,

> Verily, verily, I say unto you, He that believeth on me, the works that I do shall he do also; and greater works than these shall he do; because I go unto my Father.

The anointing on Jesus that enabled Jesus to make others whole has been given to us. Jesus told us to go into the world and preach the gospel, to heal the sick and cast out demons.

God wants his body to be whole in the last days, that we may deliver a potent dose of his Spirit and power on the earth.

The Lord Jesus promised that we do the works that he did and even greater works (meaning on a greater scale or greater in quantity), because what's greater than raising Lazarus who had been dead for four days? Jesus meant greater in quantity, not quality, because he's going to the Father (John 14:12). Well, he has gone to the Father, so where's the beef? What happened to the greater works? Some Christians use the excuse that it is impossible to do what Christ did because Jesus had the Spirit without measure. Let's look at this passage of scripture:

> John answered and said, "A man can receive nothing, except it be given him from heaven. Ye yourselves bear witness that I said, 'I am not the Christ, but that I am sent before him. He that has the bride is the bridegroom: but the friend of the bridegroom, which standeth, and heareth him, rejoiceth greatly because of the bridegroom's voice: this my joy therefore is fulfilled. He must increase, but I must decrease. He that cometh from above is above all: he that is of the earth is earthly, and speaketh of the earth. He that cometh from heaven is above all. And what he hath seen and heard that he testifieth; and no man receiveth his testimony. He that hath received his testimony hath set to his seal that God is true. For he whom God hath sent speaketh the words of God: for God gives not the Spirit by measure unto him." John 3:27–34 (KJV)

John was explaining that his dispensation was ending and Jesus's was beginning. Verse 34 states that he, meaning Jesus, was given the Spirit, meaning the Holy Spirit, without measure. Did Jesus declare this? No, John did; in fact, Jesus said something contrary to that particular passage: we would do greater works. How can we do greater works on a limited amount of supernatural ability of the Holy Spirit? We can't. God has equipped us all with his Spirit—not some of him, but all of him—thus enabling us to do as Jesus said, greater works. If we would learn to cut out all the religious excuses and fellowship more with the Lord in prayer, fasting, meditation, and studying of the Word, we would become a more effective and active leader in our community and even the world. This is why we need to be made whole.

God wants us whole first as an individual and collectively as a body so he can make others whole through us. By allowing him to work through us, we can minster life to those who need it. When we are converted (the Greek word is *epistrepho*, meaning immediate and decisive change consequent to deliberate choice), we must strengthen our brothers. In essence, when we are converted, turned, changed, made whole, we must strengthen our brothers. Return the favor, if you will. It is the enemy who has hindered, afflicted, oppressed, and distracted God's people from walking in the fullness of what God has called us to become. The only way we can be complete, whole, is to be hidden in God with Christ. It's time that we, the body of Christ, surrender our lives totally to Christ, thus decreasing of ourselves and allowing the Holy Spirit to complete the work in us and through us, fulfilling the last day move of God as spoken by the prophet Joel.

> And it shall come to pass afterward, that I will pour out my Spirit upon all flesh; and your sons and your daughters shall prophesy, your old men shall dream dreams, your young men shall see visions.
> Joel 2:28 (KJV)

Joel's prophesy says, as the result of God pouring out his Spirit, both men and women will prophesy (project or speak forth the Word and purpose of God), the older men will dream, and the younger will become visionaries and carry out those dreams. Awesome! In order for this to happen, we have got to be whole, we must make the proper adjustments, and in order to work toward being made whole, we must fully understand ourselves. The next chapters will deal with us (man) and how to align ourselves with his Word.

God the Father has called us to perfection (maturity). Is this attainable? Of course, why would Jesus say, "Be ye therefore perfect [or complete, whole, if you will], even as your Father in Heaven is perfect" (Matt. 5:48). With God's Spirit on the inside of us, it is attainable. It is a goal, a standard, a benchmark set by the Almighty that if we totally surrender to the leading of the Holy Spirit and obtain a greater knowledge of him ("My people perish because of lack of knowledge") through the Word of God, obedience, and prayer, we can be made whole, and then and only then may we take our position in the kingdom of God and fulfill our purpose. Hallelujah!

# Chapter 2

## Whole but Separate

In the book of Genesis chapter 1 verse 26 (CEV), God said,

> God said, "Now we will make humans, and they will be like us. We will let them rule the fish, the birds, and all other living creatures."

God created us in the image and likeness of himself. He created us with a purpose in mind, and that is to be fruitful and exercise the same authority his Son, Jesus, did in the earth.

God is triune or tripartite. Simply put, he is three in one, constituting a trinity in unity as the Godhead. When he said "Let us," he was not conferring with the angels or the beast around the throne. He was speaking to the Son (Jesus) and the Holy Spirit. God is triune, and so are we. Each part of the trinity is represented in us. We have an eternal spirit. Yes, we are a spirit. Although we spend the majority of our time catering to the needs, wants, and desires of the flesh, we are a spirit, and the moment that spirit leaves our body, we are gone. Our flesh starts to decompose, and the eternal components are transferred from time into eternity. We also have an eternal soul, which is encased in what now is a temporary body. God is a spirit. He is, was, and always will be the Supreme Being, Divine Creator, Elohim. He is omnipresent, meaning he is present everywhere at once. He is omnipotent, which means he has unlimited power. He is omniscient, meaning he knows all things. God has a body representing Christ, the Word that was made flesh and dwelt among us. God has a spirit, soul, and body. We have a spirit, soul, and body. These three components make up the creature we know as man. We will get a little deeper in these components throughout the book. The reason we don't understand God is that we don't understand ourselves. We (mankind) are very interesting beings. David said in Psalm 139:14 (KJV),

> I will praise thee; for I am fearfully and wonderfully made: marvelous are thy works; and that my soul knoweth right well.

Here, David is praising God for making him, yet he referred to his soul knowing right, or fully, well. David realized he was not just mere clay but a well-crafted creation that is designed after God's image and likeness. A special creation of God created for a specific purpose.

The Bible declares that we are created in the image and likeness of God. Let's turn to the book of Genesis, the book of beginnings, to get a clear picture. Genesis 1:26 (NKJV) reads,

> Then God said, "Let us make man in Our image, according to Our likeness; let them have dominion over the fish of the sea, and over the birds of the air, and over the cattle, over all the earth, and over every creeping thing that creeps on the earth."

Was he talking to the angels? No! Was he talking to himself? Yes! But God is not crazy! He was talking to Jesus, who was in his bosom. John 1:18 (NKJV) reads,

> No one has seen God at any time. The only begotten Son, who is *"in the bosom"* of the Father, He has declared Him.

The Holy Ghost, who moved back and forth over the water and created everything at God's command, is God the Holy Spirit, the third person of the Godhead.

> And the earth was without form, and void; and darkness was on the face of the deep. And the Spirit of God was hovering over the face of the waters. Genesis 1:2 (NKJV)

God is one yet separate. Let us look at a couple of scriptures:

> Hear, O Israel: The Lord our God, the Lord is one.
> Deuteronomy 6:4 (NIV)

> Just as Jesus was coming up out of the water, he saw
> heaven being torn open and the Spirit descending
> on Him like a dove. And a voice came from heaven:
> "You are my Son, whom I love; with you I am well
> pleased." Mark 1:10–11 (NIV)

In Deuteronomy 6:4, Israel declares he is one but united, Elohim, the plural name; however, in Mark's account, we see God is separated: Jesus being baptized, the Holy Spirit descending on Jesus in the form of a dove, and the Father (El) declaring his love and approval for Jesus from heaven. By the way, the Holy Spirit is the same Holy Spirit who dwells in us and is waiting to move through us, to lead us, and to comfort us, etc. But we'll discuss the ministry of the Holy Ghost in another chapter. Let's take a look at Genesis chapter 2 verse 7 (KJV):

> And the Lord God formed man of the dust of the
> ground, and breathed into his nostrils the breath of
> life; and man became a living soul.

Let's see how God made man. The Bible declares that God formed man from the dust of the ground and breathed in his nostrils the breath of life, the soul; the Greek word is *psuche* meaning "the breath of life." The word *soul* has various meanings. This particular passage is used to describe an animate creature, human or other. Although the scripture uses the word *soul* in our translation, it is not directly referring to the soul; it is stating that man is a living being, having both soul and spirit.

Only man has a soul; animals have a spirit but no soul. Angels are called ministering spirits. God wants to inhabit our spirit and soul to lead, convict, convince, and comfort. Unlike a demonic possession, they (demons) can possess a body to control because they are fallen angels, and so is Lucifer. They are spirit beings (see Isaiah 14:12); however, man is created in the image and likeness of God. Man has a spirit, soul, and body. Each part of the Trinity, or Godhead, is represented in man. You are a spirit representing the Holy Spirit, or the Spirit of God. You have a soul, which consists of your mind, will, and emotions. They all make up your individuality, or persona, representing the Almighty God, the Supreme Being, El, and a body representing Jesus. Yes, we are fearfully and wonderfully made. That's why there's a need for man to understand himself and line up each component with the Word of God. In the past, man has failed to understand himself; thus, he has been crippled in fulfilling God's will for his life. By becoming preoccupied with ourselves, the cares of this life, future goals, dreams, and aspirations, our focal point has been our needs, whether they be spiritual, psychological, physical, sociological, or financial. The Bible says that we ought to look to Jesus, the author and finisher of our faith (Hebrews 12:2, KJV). The more we focus on Jesus, the more God's prearranged purpose for our lives can be revealed to us and through his Word and prayer, and then and only then will we find inner peace. Isaiah 55:2 (NKJV) reads,

> Why do you spend money on what is not bread, and wages on what does not satisfy? Listen carefully to Me, and eat what is good, and let your soul delight itself in abundance.

Many people are desperately trying to find peace through the things of this world and are still not satisfied when God is offering a satisfying life through his Son, Jesus; his presence; his Spirit within; and the Word. They simply need to make the necessary adjustments. Yes, that's right. You must receive the regeneration of your spirit, renew your soul (mind, will, and emotions) with the Word of God, and crucify and mortify your flesh in order to become subject to the Word of God and not the affairs of this world. Matthew 6:33 (KJV) reads,

> But seek ye first the kingdom of God, and his righteousness; and all these things shall be added unto you.

What things? Things like food, clothing, housing, companionship, etc. (i.e., the cares of this life.) When we begin to worry, it's a sure sign of not being made whole. Jesus had one care, and that was to do the will of the one who sent him (John 4:34, KJV). We must pursue God's will, and while in pursuit of God's will, God will in turn perfect, make whole, and complete those things that concern us, and the means by which we get out of this dilemma is by dissecting ourselves and lining up each component with the Word of God. Yes, we can be more like Jesus! Isn't that exciting?

We must begin to learn to examine ourselves in order to discern what component is the most dominant. Is it our flesh? Is it our spirit? Is it our soul? Well, if our flesh is more dominant than our soul and spirit, that makes us a carnal Christian. If we are allowing our soul to be more dominant, then we tend to become more double-minded and tend to reason away the promises of God if we don't renew our minds. Many times, someone completes the initial conversion. They receive the new birth; however, they can't seem to understand why they are still struggling. What they don't realize is that although their spirit is reborn, their soul, or mind, has to be renewed daily by the Word of God through positive confessions and meditation.

> For the word of God is living and powerful, and sharper than any two-edged sword, piercing even to the division of the soul and the spirit, and of the joints and marrow, and is the discerner of the thoughts and intents of the heart. Hebrews 4:12 (NKJV)

It is expedient that we take the living Word of God in our spirit and apply the proper scripture in the proper context to the proper component. God's Word also has the ability to dissect and address every component with issues and can also reveal to us the basis for our intentions. The Word of God can meet your spiritual, emotional, sociological, and psychological needs. A daily dose of his Word and prayer is just the remedy we need for life's issues.

It's vital for our spiritual growth and development to know our full makeup and how to dissect and apply the scriptures to our spirit, soul, and body. In the next three chapters, we will address each component individually and describe each component's purpose and how to apply the appropriate scriptures to fortify each component. This will aid in your spiritual growth and development, thus moving you closer to perfection or wholeness. You should be ecstatic; I know I am.

# Chapter 3

## The Spirit: The Reborn Component

Now we begin with the most important component of man: the spirit. As I shared in previous chapters, mankind is made up of three components: the spirit, the soul, and the body. The spirit is defined by Dictionary.com as "The principle of conscious life; the vital principle in humans, animating the body or mediating between body and soul. The incorporeal part of humans: present in spirit though absent in body." We are a spirit. We have a soul, and both are encased in a body. We are spirit beings. We are eternal spirit beings created in God's image and likeness. What is that likeness, you may ask? We are eternal spirit beings like the Father who created us. One may argue by saying, "Then why do men, women, and children die every day?" When we die as the world says, what really happens is our spirit and soul are transferred from the natural, earthly realm to the spiritual realm, from *chronos* to *aionios*, or from time to eternity. The spirit never dies. The body simply can no longer exist in *chronos*, or time. The spirit and soul are eternal, while this earthly body is temporary, or temporal. That flesh we see in a casket is nothing more than an empty shell of the Father's creation. The body is merely the earth suit. It is nothing more than a temporary housing unit for the spirit and the soul. As soon as the spirit and soul exits the body, it (the body) begins to decay.

If you wanted to scuba dive, you would need a wet suit and scuba gear to survive underwater. The same is true if you were to walk around on the moon; you would need a space suit. In order to exist on earth, you need your body. Despite all the time and effort we put into making the flesh look good, it doesn't last forever, and it still will pass away. It was once designed to last forever; however, as a result of sin, it decays.

The good news is God the Father, Jehovah Jireh, has already prepared an eternal body for us. It is so important that we must dedicate the eternal components (the spirit and the soul) to God's presence and his Word and keep this temporary component (the flesh) in check by making it succumb to God's will and the Word, which is his expressed will.

The book of Revelation states that those who lived and were eternally condemned were cast into the lake of fire; this is the second death (Revelation 20:14). The second death John was referring to is a sentencing of eternal damnation or being banished eternally from the presence of God. So whether in heaven or hell, paradise or Hades, lake of fire or new Jerusalem, you will still exist forever! There is no "When you're dead, you're done." Your spirit and soul will spend eternity somewhere. That is why it is imperative that you align your spirit, soul, and body with the Word of God.

The spirit of man is where the new birth, or the first baptism, begins. There are several baptisms: the baptism into Christ, or the new birth; the baptism of water; the baptism of the Holy Spirit; and the baptism of fire, just to name a few, but that will be in my next book. The baptism into Christ is when the Spirit of God literally transforms your spirit and makes it sensitive to the will, voice, and conviction of God. It reads in 2 Corinthians 5:17 (KJV),

> If any man be in Christ, he is a new creature: old things are passed away; behold, all things are become new.

This is not a figurative statement; the Lord transforms or makes your spirit sin-sensitive in the new birth. Before you received Jesus as Lord of your life, you were able to sin liberally without giving it a second thought. I love the Message Bible's translation of this passage:

> Now we look inside, and what we see is that anyone united with the Messiah gets a fresh start, is created new. The old life is gone; a new life burgeons! Look at it. 2 Corinthians 5:17 (MSG)

Yes, let's look at it. Let's look at what literally happens. Immediately following the reception of Jesus the Messiah as your personal savior, you start to develop a sin consciousness; you start to become sin-sensitive, convicted whenever you're found doing sinful things. This happens to everyone who receives the new birth. God initiates the spiritual metamorphosis, and you start to evolve into a spiritually conscious, spiritually sensitive being. You begin feeling godly sorrowful. Whenever you commit sin, there is a constant reminder, a silent alarm inside of you that detects the presence of sin and convicts you to do what is right. You were once able to sin and go to bed and not lose one night's sleep; now, you can't rest until you make amends with both God and man. The scriptures says,

> The heart is deceitful above all things, and desperately wicked; who can know it? Jeremiah 17:9 (NKJV)

We (mankind) were born in sin and shaped in iniquity. In addition, Satan is always sending offenses in order to contaminate our heart (spirit). Even after the transformation at the new birth, we still need to decontaminate our spirit and also protect it from future contamination. Satan will send people, places, and things into your life for one reason and one reason only, and that is to contaminate your spirit. Only the Word of God and the power of the Holy Spirit can decontaminate our spirit. Everything we do or say stems from our spirit. It may have crossed your mind, but by the time you act on it, whether verbally, physically, or emotionally, it has stemmed from your spirit. Jesus said, out of the abundance of the heart (spirit), the mouth speaks.

God communicates with us through our spirit, not our mind. He leads us by his Spirit, who communicates to us through our spirit. Oh, and by the way, the next time you realize you've missed the Father's leading, don't say, "Something told me . . ." It's not something, but it is *someone*. The Word of God reads in Proverbs 20:27 (KJV),

The spirit of man is the candle of the Lord.

The Contemporary English Version reads like this:

Our inner thoughts are a lamp from the Lord, and they search our hearts.

This passage refers to the inner thoughts. It could have easily said "our mind," but it says the inner thoughts beyond the recesses of your mind, your spirit. God longs for the opportunity to converse, commune, and capacitate or charge you in his presence daily. The book of Genesis informs us that God came down in the cool of the day to commune or walk with Adam. How much more does he desire to commune or fellowship with us daily. For most of us, the reason we struggle with our faith is because we have cut off our line of communication with the Father. I'm not saying you are not born again, but you have abandoned your special scheduled "cool of the day" prayer life. Let's take a look at Luke18:1 (NKJV):

Then He spoke a parable to them, that, men [mankind] always ought to pray and not lose heart.

Meditating on the Word of God and praying are vital for your spiritual survival. We are constantly bombarded with various trials, tests, and temptations daily, and as our faith level diminishes, we need to refuel in the presence of the Father. When I was a kid, we played with glow sticks; they were these plastic tubes filled with this neon-green liquid and a glass vial inside that, when the inner vial was crushed, mixed with the neon-green fluid and caused it to glow in the dark. After a while though, the glow stick would start to become dull and would lose its glow, but we would just hold it over a lightbulb for a few minutes, and the glow stick would shine just bright as before. That's a lot like our new birth encounter with God. When we ask Jesus into our heart, or our spirit, the inner vial is broken, and we start to glow. We are excited about becoming a new creature and receiving the new birth, but then Satan comes with various attacks, and you start to lose your glow. But if we can get in the presence of God, then we can be rejuvenated and continue to shine as bright as before. Whenever we feel spiritually empty, we must refuel in the presence of the Father. We cannot remain spiritually strong outside of the presence of the Father. David said,

> You will show me the path of life; in Your presence
> is fullness of joy; at Your right hand are pleasures
> forevermore. Psalm 16:11 (NKJV)

Whenever you are low on joy and hope, you need his presence. Whenever you need protection and confidence, you need his presence. David declares the following in Psalm 91:1–2 (NKJV).

He who dwells in the secret place of the Most High [Elohim] shall abide under the shadow of the Almighty [El Shaddai]. I will say of the LORD, "He is my refuge and my fortress; My God, in Him I will trust."

David realized that the Father's presence was his source of joy, hope, and confidence. The Father's presence is still the main source of hope, joy, and confidence. His presence restores, revitalizes, and rejuvenates us, enabling us to get through life victoriously as we complete his predestined purpose for our lives. Hallelujah!

The strategy of Satan is to shut down our line of communication with the Father by contaminating our spirit through various offenses (trials, tests, and temptations). While we are distracted by thoughts of "Who hurt me," "Who talked about me," "Who betrayed me," "But he or she said they would never leave me," etc., your spirit life has gone to the dogs. While we are distracted by Satan's fiery darts, we are not praying or meditating or reading the Word or attending church regularly. In other words, our spiritual life diminishes if we allow it.

First of all, let me address certain offenses. About 80 percent of all offenses involves someone. They are relational or stem from relationships. The Word of God declares that we should not lean (depend) on the arm of flesh. What that simply means is that we should not put our stock (faith) in man or even our own resources, but what the Word of God does tell us is to depend totally on him and his resources. If we would only realize that man will be man and are liable to disappoint us from time to time, whether it be intentionally or inadvertently, then we must forgive, forget, and move on! If you are ever to see a crime scene, you would see the yellow crime scene tape, numbered cards counting bullet casings, and other various pieces of evidence or maybe a body that is covered up, but most of all, you would see police officers handling crowd control, saying the following, "Move along, there is nothing to see here!" That is the one phrase that I use to get through various offenses that involve man. We have a choice whether to keep staring at the crime scenes of life (offenses) or move along because there is nothing to see there. There is nothing beneficial to us at the crime scene. I used to worry about what people said about me. I especially worried when they would tell lies about me then one day while reading the Word of God, I saw the passage where the Pharisees called Jesus a bibber (an alcoholic), and the Lord spoke to me and said, "If they told lies about me, they are going to tell lies about you. Are you better than me?" Then he led me to the following two passages:

Blessed are you when people insult you, persecute you and falsely say all kinds of evil against you because of Me. Matthew 5:11 (NIV)

These things I have spoken to you, that you may have peace. In this world you will have tribulation; but be of good cheer, I have overcome the world. John 16:33 (NKJV)

Needless to say, I have been fine ever since. I later found out that the Amplified Bible defines the word *blessed* and notes in parentheses the words *happy, fortunate, to be envied* after the word *bless* throughout that translation. We are blessed. Some of us know, while others tend to forget. We are happy not because we believe everything is all right all the time but because we are confident that whenever anything does go awry, we know a God who can make the crooked places straight and the rough places smooth. We are fortunate because the doors that are closed for everyone else will open for us, and one true indicator of being blessed is the presence of the haters, or the sudden increase of those who envy you. So we need to be delivered from people, including ourselves, because we can tend to be a little too self-reliant at times, and that will solve the people problem. I'm not saying that we should go through life in a pseudo schizophrenic state, where we are suspicious of everyone and unable to trust anyone. We can trust others; however, we must trust God more. We cannot let the offenses caused by others startle and devastate us like it has never happened to us before. There is nothing to reflect on, just give, forgive, and move along. Give it to God, forgive the offender, and move along! Then there is the other 20 percent that is more situational (sickness, finances, depression, etc.), give those problems to God because he is the only one who can fix it anyway. In the Amplified translation of 1 Peter 5:7, the Word of God says,

Casting the whole of your cares [all of you fears, doubts and worries] once and for all on the Lord for He cares about you affectionately and sees about you watchfully.

If we are ever going to become victorious in this Christian walk, we have to be able to stop staring at the situation and *move along.*

We must keep our spirits cleansed from contamination and not build our lives and belief system on past bad experiences. It is good to learn from the past experiences, both good and bad, but here is what we must do in order to maintain good heart (spirit) health.

1.  Pray and ask God to cleanse our hearts of any spiritual contaminants (sin, hurts, disappointments, and other offenses). The scripture says, "Therefore, having these promises, beloved let us cleanse ourselves from all filthiness of the flesh and spirit, perfecting holiness in the fear of God." We must ask the Lord to cleanse us from everything that would keep us from going forward and getting closer to God. David wrote,

    > Create in me a clean heart, O God, and renew a steadfast spirit within me. Psalm 51:10 (NKJV)

We must allow God to remove all past offenses that may have altered our path or right perspective in life and put us back in the right path and restore the right perspective. That will result in what David said in verse 12: the restoration of the joy of our salvation. Have you lost the joy of your salvation? That is a sure sign that your spirit is contaminated. In the natural realm, if the human heart is filled with plaque, it cannot function properly. Neither can the spirit function properly if it is contaminated with sin and offenses. *We must decontaminate!*

2. Once cleansed, we must guard, garrison, and protect our hearts from future contamination. Proverbs 4:23 (NKJV) reads,

> Keep your heart with all diligence, For
> out of it springs the issues of life.

How we think, what we speak, and how we govern ourselves all flow from our hearts (spirit), and allowing the wrong things into our hearts can totally transform our life. *We must protect our spirits from future contaminants!* This will allow us to be able to receive wholeness in our lives as well as assist others in doing so. Hallelujah! We must use the tools God gave us to be made whole—his Word and his Spirit. Psalm 119:11 (NKJV) reads,

> Your word I have hidden in my heart that I might
> not sin against you.

We must remove out of our spirit all the contamination of sin and offenses from the past and the present. In addition, we must protect ourselves from all future contamination. This is why the apostle Paul urged us to put on the whole armor of God. It is the breastplate of righteousness that protects us from all condemnation from both Satan and man. Knowing that we have the righteousness of God in Christ Jesus gives us the confidence and self-worth to stand in faith and overcome the past, present, and future challenges of life with a pure heart. Say this prayer with me.

Father, in the name of Jesus, I come into your presence, asking you to create in me a clean heart and renew a steadfast spirit within me. I have allowed the enemy to contaminate my heart, but your Word says that if I confess my sin, you have the power to not only forgive but cleanse (decontaminate) my spirit. I forgive everyone who has offended me because I am aware that if I don't forgive men their trespasses, you won't forgive me of my trespasses. Thank you, Lord, for cleansing my spirit of all the contaminants that would prevent me from drawing closer to you and fulfilling my purpose in this world. Now I can become who you have called me to be. Amen.

# Chapter 4

## The Soul: The Renewed Component

I explained in the previous chapter that we are triune like the Godhead. There are three parts that make up the whole man. We are a spirit, we have a soul, and both are encased in a body. We are now going to address the second component: the soul. The soul is defined as the emotional part of human nature, the seat of the feelings or sentiments. The soul is the nerve center of man. It is the part of man that gives man his or her individuality. There are three areas of the soul: the mind, the will, and the emotions. Generically, the mind is simply your mental capacity, your IQ, or level of intelligence. This level of intelligence varies from person to person. Some have more of an academic aptitude, while others may have more common sense. This is one level of individuality in which the Father uses to give each one of us our uniqueness. However, the mind, as I mentioned earlier, is a battlefield of *all* thoughts, suggestions, or ideas. Then there is the will or the drive or intent of man. This area causes some to be more passive, while others are more aggressive. It is the area where some of us are ambitious, while others are cautious. It is why some are self-motivators, self-starters, while others rely on others to motivate them. Some people are strong willed, while others are easily persuaded. Some rise up and become leaders, while others are followers. It all is an extension of the will. Then there are the emotions. This area of the soul is where the moods and temperaments are found. The mind is the filter of the soul. It is the battlefield of all thoughts, suggestions, ideas, and inspirations, whether good or evil.

The mind receives signals from our five senses; I call them receptors. It process the signal, coordinates how to respond to that signal, then determines which emotion to use in accordance with the response. Let's say you hear a balloon pop. The mind receives a signal from the ears, and almost immediately, you jump as you momentarily experience the emotion of fear. Fear is defined as an emotion aroused by impeding danger, evil, pain, etc. Let's say you're at a baseball game, and the batter swings at a pitch and accidently releases the bat. You see the bat headed toward your head; your mind coordinates with your will to duck as your emotions stimulate a brief feeling of fear in less than a nanosecond.

Satan tries to infiltrate the mind through the senses! Let's say you are getting ready to go to church when the phone rings, and a fellow parishioner tells you about how difficult their day went and that they don't think they're going to make it to church while they suggest to you that you must be exhausted as well. You begin to ponder on the conversation. Your will to go to church gets altered, and you conclude, "I think I'll stay home too." Or maybe you hear gossip about a close friend from another parishioner, and now you feel a little uncomfortable around that friend and begin to distance yourself from them. In each case, the mind processed the information, coordinated with your will and emotion, and devised a response. That's how it works. This is why we need to dissect each component and make it subject to the Word of God. Remember, the spirit is reborn; however, the mind must be renewed. Most people are under the impression that the spirit and the soul are one and the same; however, the Word of God expresses a distinction between soul and spirit. Hebrews 4:12 (NKJV) reads this way:

> For the word God is living and powerful and sharper than any two edged sword, piercing even to the division of the *soul and the spirit* and of the joints and the marrow, and is a discerner of the thoughts and intents of the heart.

Here we see clearly in the Word of God a distinction between the spirit and soul. They are two different, distinct, and unique components, and the scripture tells us that the Word of God is the agent used to divide the two. We must allow the Word of God to dissect that we may apply the right Word remedy for the right component. You don't apply eyedrops in the ear, nor do you place eardrops in your nose. There are scriptures that address every component of man, and we must implement or apply the proper scriptures to the right components.

We must rightly divide the Word, and that not only means placing the Word in its proper context but also applying it to the right component of man and thereby living a life that meets the Father's approval. When we are born again, our soul is not saved yet. Romans 10:9–10 (NKJV) reads,

> That if you confess with your mouth the Lord Jesus and believe in your heart that God has raised Him from the dead, you will be saved. For with the heart one believes unto righteousness, and with the mouth confession is made unto salvation.

When you receive the baptism into Christ, your spirit is reborn. However, the soul has to be saved or renewed daily by the Word of God. We are like used computers; we must delete or deprogram from the memory (soul) and hard drive (spirit) the previous owner's programs and upload on the hard drive the programs that we desire in order for it to become our personal computer. The same holds true with us as believers; we must rid ourselves of the old program of sin and death while uploading the Word of God. This is what makes our relationship with God personal, because what's on my memory is not the same programs that's stored on your memory. Satan was our previous owner, and he placed all sorts of sinful things on the memory of our souls. Although we have been born again, we still are found to possess evil thoughts, attitudes, and behaviors on our memory that are not suitable to the new owner (God). We must erase or delete from our memory (soul) before it gets stored on our hard drive (spirit) the previous owner Satan's program. It reads in 2 Corinthians 10:5 (NKJV),

> Casting down arguments and every high thing that exalts itself against the knowledge of God, bringing every thought into captivity to the obedience of Christ.

That is the process of deprogramming and uploading. This is not only for our transformation and the actual saving of our souls but it also enables us to receive, process, and allow in our spirit what is wholesome and right. In 1 Corinthians 2:15–16 (NKJV), it reads,

> But he who is spiritual judges all things, yet he is rightly judged by no one. For "who has known the mind of the LORD that he may instruct Him?" But we have the mind of Christ.

We must delete all our thoughts that are not pleasing to the Father, those thoughts that bring about those animalistic impulses that result in us acting out of character and, committing sin. We must cast down those thoughts, imaginations, or suggestions that are in opposition to the precepts, concepts, and commandments of God. Satan is constantly sending viruses—the Bible refers to those viruses as "fiery darts of the wicked" in Ephesians 6:16 (KJV)—in an attempt to bring condemnation and thereby sifting your faith in the Lord until there is no faith left. I want to take a moment to expound on the armor of God, not all pieces, but two pieces in particular: the helmet of salvation and the shield of faith. The helmet is designed to protect the soldier from any head trauma he or she may encounter during battle. Unlike the natural armor, the spiritual armor, once adorned, must never be taken off. Why? Because the battle for your soul is constant and continuous. The helmet convicts and convinces you of your salvation from both eternal damnation and every adverse situation you will ever face in this life. You need the shield of faith because it is faith (belief coupled with a corresponding action) that enables you to be courageous and confident enough to speak the Word of God and God's desired result over every situation and circumstance, thereby defusing or thwarting the strategies and stratagems of the enemy. We place the helmet on and keep it on by meditating on the Word of God daily. Joshua 1:8 (AMPC) reads,

> This Book of the Law shall not depart out of your mouth, but you shall *meditate on it day and night, that you may observe to do according to all that is written in it. For then you will make your way prosperous, and then you shall deal wisely and have good success.*

This passage explains the point I'm trying to make in this whole chapter, and that is if we keep the Word of God in our mind, it will transform our will and emotions. Our animalistic urges will diminish, and our impulses will line up with the Word of God. The will to sin will decrease as it is replaced by a willingness to please

God. Our former emotions will dissipate as it is replaced by the fruit of the Spirit. Our desire to obey the Word of God increases as the desire to sin decreases, and as a result of our obedience, God rewards us with prosperity and good success. So in conclusion, in the book of Philippians, we are instructed to think on certain things, and they are as follows:

> Finally, brethren, whatever things are true, whatever things are noble, whatever things are just, whatever things are pure, whatever things are lovely, whatever things are of good report, if there is any virtue and if there is anything praiseworthy—meditate on these things. Philippians 4:8 (NKJV)

There is only one thing that meets *all* the qualities described in the above scripture, and that is the Word of God. We are called to meditate on the Word and confess and profess it *daily!* What we hear ourselves declare in the earth becomes our reality. Have you ever told a lie so much that you forgot the truth? Whatever we hear the most becomes our reality, truth or lie. The Bible says faith comes by hearing. Well, so does fear, doubt, and disbelief. It is imperative that we flood our mind and spirit with the Word of God. Meditation allows the Word to seep into our spirit, and the Holy Spirit will bring it back to our remembrance when needed, similar to how the cloud holds on to your old files on your computer. This will help to keep you walking in faith. Yes, we are fearfully and wonderfully made indeed.

# Chapter 5

## The Body: The Crucified Component

In this chapter, we are going to focus on the body. Once again, I'll start by saying that we are triune, or tripartite, beings. The prefix *tri-* means "three," then *partite* means "parts or components." We consist of three parts: spirit, soul, and body. As I stated in a previous chapter, we are spirit beings; in fact, the spirit is the real you, the eternal you. The second component is the soul. The soul has three components, and they are the mind, the will, and the emotions. The soul is the component that determines your intellect, behavioral tendencies, your will, as well as emotional makeup. Your soul gives your individuality, and it is the battlefield of *all* thoughts, both good and evil. It receives, processes, and devises a response for every thought, suggestion, etc. The body is the temporary housing, or earth suit. It is where your spirit and soul lives. Like I also stated earlier, we are a spirit that has a soul, and the body is our earth suit. If you were to go to the moon, you would need a space suit. If you were to go scuba diving, you would need scuba gear. If you are going to exist on the earth, you need a body. The body was originally designed to last forever; however, because of sin as a result of the fall of man, it now deteriorates daily. The good news is when our spirit and soul are separated from the body, the Lord has promised us another body that *never* deteriorates, gets sick, afflicted, or dies. In 2 Corinthians 5:1–3 (AMPC), it reads like this,

> For we know if the tent which is our earthly home is destroyed (dissolved), we have from God a building, a house not made with hands, eternal in the heavens. Here indeed, in this [present abode, body], we sigh and groan inwardly, because we yearn to be clothed over [we yearn to put on our celestial body like a garment, to be fitted out] with our heavenly dwelling, So that by putting it on we may not be found naked (without a body).

This is why I refer to the body as a temporary housing unit. It temporarily houses the spirit and the soul. So the next time you begin to get a little discouraged about getting old and the deterioration of this outer shell, take delight in knowing that God's got another house already prepared awaiting us in heaven. One that never gets ill or dies and, most of all, not under the curse of sin and death. Hallelujah! That's something to look forward to. We must cast down or reject *every* negative thought, idea, or suggestion given to us by Satan, being ever mindful that our mind is the battlefield. The mind is the entryway of every thought, idea, or suggestion, both good and evil. We must filter out all the evil and hold on to what is good. The scripture says,

Test all things; hold fast what is good. Abstain from
every form of evil. 1 Thessalonians 5:21–22 (NKJV)

We must practice abstinence not just from fornication but from
every sinful act. We must abstain from every form of evil. This
passage is so clear and concise in any translation. Test or evaluate
every thought, hold on to the good thoughts, suggestions, or ideas,
discard the evil thoughts, suggestions, or ideas.

The god of this world's system, the devil, has devised a strategy
that keeps man focused on self-gratification. In fact, the phrase
"Do what thou wilt" is the mantra of the satanic church and the
world today. When we utilize the term "the flesh," we are referring
to a sinful nature. The Amplified Bible refers to the sin nature as
animal impulses. It is not the actual flesh itself but the sin nature
manifesting through the flesh. We see the influences of the sin
nature carried out by the flesh; thus we say it is the flesh. The body
or flesh carries out whatever responses or actions that seem more
favorable to itself. Whatever behavior we see in our lives and those
we encounter is a result of the state of the spirit and soul. If the soul
allows the sin nature to dominate the mind, will, and emotions
to the extent that the spirit becomes contaminated, a fleshly or
sinful nature will manifest. When we say someone is walking
in the flesh, what we are really saying is that the person, for the
moment, is allowing his or her flesh to gravitate to the influences
of the world and not the Word of God. We *must* not allow any
ungodly influences to infiltrate our mind, manipulate our will, or
alter our emotions. We also *must* not allow our spirit to become

contaminated. The flesh will only manifest or demonstrate what is dominating your spirit and soul, either the new life in Christ or the old man, that old sinful nature. The apostle Paul wrote,

> I have been crucified with Christ [in Him I have shared His crucifixion]; it is no longer I who live, but Christ (the Messiah) lives in me; and the life that I now live in the body I live by the faith in (by adherence to and reliance on and complete trust in) the Son of God, Who loved me and gave Himself up for me. Galatians 2:20 (AMPC)

When we allow the presence of God, the Word of God, and the influence of the Holy Spirit to control our lives, we are crucifying the flesh, or the old sinful nature. There is no physical affliction of the body but a nullifying of the sin nature. Colossians 3:5 (AMPC) reads,

> So kill (deaden, deprive of power) the evil lurking in your members [those animal impulses and all that is earthly in you that is employed in sin]: sexual vice, impurity, sensual appetites, unholy desires, and all greed and covetousness, for that is idolatry (the deifying of self and other created things instead of God).

The apostle Paul was not talking about a killing of the natural body but the sin nature, a deadening or depriving of the flesh, of the evil that lurks in our body. The apostle Paul knew all too well the struggle of the flesh versus the renewed soul and the reborn spirit. Let's look at this passage.

> For we know that the law is spiritual, but I am carnal, sold under sin. For what I am doing I do not understand. For what I will [want] to do, that I do not practice; but what I hate, that I do. If then, I do what I will not to do, I agree with the law that it is good. Romans 7:14–16 (NKJV)

This is interesting. Here we have the apostle Paul, the apostle of the gentile believers and writer of three quarters of the New testament, confessing that he is struggling with doing what is right. Oh my! The truth is that we *all* face the same struggles daily; no one is exempt. Paul discovered something that we all need to discover. Let's look a little further.

> *But now*, it is no longer I who do it, but sin that dwells in me. For I know that in me *(that is in my flesh)* nothing good dwells; for to will [the want to] is present with me, but how to perform what is good I do not find. For the good I will [want] to do, I do not do; but the evil I will [want] not to do, that I practice. Now if I do what I will [want] not to do, it is no longer I who do it, but the sin that dwells in me. Romans 7:17–20 (NKJV)

The apostle Paul realized then the same thing that we are experiencing now, and that is despite the new birth experience, being sin conscious, and having a desire to submit to the Lord, his presence, and his Word, we still find ourselves doing exactly what we no longer want to do. Before the new birth, we could sin and not lose one moment's sleep. Now we are frustrated because we find it difficult sometimes to do the good we want to do. Many people have even given up and backslidden because they didn't understand that sin is still present in their body, and although their spirit is reborn, their soul has to be saved through the Word of God, Spirit of God, and the presence of God. We need to spend time in God's presence, fellowshipping with his Spirit in addition to time in God's Word, to aid us in the domination and control of this fleshly body. Paul was able to dissect himself and conclude that although his spirit was reborn and his soul was being deprogrammed and reprogrammed, there was another law on the inside:

> I find then *a law*, that evil is present with me, the one who wills to do good. For I delight in the law of God according to the inward man [the spirit]. But I see another law warring against the law of *my mind* and bringing me into captivity. Romans 7:21-23 (NKJV)

Paul realized that although he was born again and had received the new birth and his soul was under reconstruction, that didn't eliminate the mental attacks of Satan via thoughts, ideas, or suggestions. Situations in life can also contribute to the infiltration of the soul and, eventually, contamination of the spirit. Paul mentioned that there was another law that was warring against the law of the reconstruction or deprogramming and reprogramming of his mind. He later revealed in chapter 8 verse 2 that the other law was the law of sin and death. This simply means that even after our conversion, Satan doesn't stop sending evil or sinful thoughts, ideas, and suggestions. Some people are under the impression that the moment that they're born again, Satan stops his attack and the only voice you will hear is Jesus's, and when that doesn't happen, they tend to question their salvation. Some people turn back as a result of not knowing the Word or themselves and aligning themselves with the Word. We must dissect ourselves and properly apply the Word to our spirit, soul. This will enable us to subdue this sinful nature, or the flesh. Let's look a little further down in this passage,

> O wretched man I am! Who can save me from this
> body of death? I thank God—through Jesus Christ
> or Lord! Romans 7:24–25 (NKJV)

When many of us read this passage, it seems that the apostle Paul was admitting defeat and that there is no remedy to that other law in our members that is warring against the law of our mind. Paul was not admitting defeat, but in verse 24, he was merely describing the feeling that both he and every believer feels after yielding to sin. The frustration and feeling of defeat brought on as a result of guilt and shame. The aftereffects of sin brought on by Satan. The Amplified Bible reads like this,

> O unhappy and pitiable and wretched man that I am! Who will release and deliver me from [the shackles of] this body of death? Romans 7:24 (AMPC)

After we have given into the other law (the law of sin and death), guilt and shame follows as Satan attempts to overwhelm you with condemnation. You feel unhappy, pitiable, and yes, of course, wretched. We feel the distance resulting from sin, which separates us from God; however, we must remember though that before the new birth, we didn't feel this wretchedness because we were already condemned.

I worked twenty-nine and a half years in law enforcement as a correctional officer and the majority of that time in the court services unit. I was responsible for transporting inmates back and forth to court. While I was there, I saw some inmates sentenced to the death penalty. The judge would say to the defendant (inmate), "I condemn you to die." That prisoner would be devastated. Before receiving Jesus, we were already condemned to eternal damnation, the second death, but thanks to God, Jesus came and expunged or blotted out our record. Hallelujah! Now that we are new creatures in Christ, Satan tempts us to commit sin, thereby enabling him to attempt to layer us with a shroud of guilt, condemnation, and death. Paul was certainly not admitting defeat, just letting us know that everyone, including himself, was facing the same spiritual attack. He was letting us know the aftereffects of guilt and shame is commonplace to every believer, but he was not waving the white flag of surrender, no, not at all. Let's take a look at verse 25 in the Amplified translation.

> Oh thank God! [He will!] through Jesus Christ (the Anointed One) our Lord! So then indeed I, of myself with the mind and heart, serve the Law of God, but with the flesh the law of sin. Romans 7:25 (AMPC)

So here we see that Paul gave glory to God because of his Son, Jesus, who has and will erase our sins, past, present, and future. In addition to that, he declared something that both he and all of us must do to overcome sin, and that is to serve the law of God with both our mind and heart (spirit and soul) and avoid serving sin in or with the flesh (sin nature). The flesh is an enemy of God. How is this accomplished? It is accomplished by becoming whole, dissecting yourself and applying the Word of God to the proper components. First off, keeping our reborn spirit from sinful contamination, or guarding our heart. Secondly, filtering or casting down all ungodly thoughts, ideas, and suggestions constantly. Let me add, as believers, we will become more successful in our Christian walk if we simply become proactive. We are called to pray the moment we are tempted and not after the flesh has carried out the sin. It is better to pray than apologize! Jesus taught the disciples to utilize prayer as a buffer against sin; however, most Christians spend most of their prayer time repenting for the sin already committed. Let's look at a couple of scriptures where Jesus spoke about being proactive in our prayer life.

> And *lead (bring) us not into temptation*, but deliver us from the evil one. For Yours is the kingdom and the power and the glory forever. Amen. Matthew 6:13 (AMPC)

> And He said to them, Why do you sleep? *Get up and pray that you may not enter [at all] into temptation.* Luke 22:46 (AMPC)

> *Watch and pray so that you will not fall into temptation.* The spirit is willing but the flesh is weak. Matthew 26:41 (NIV)

Here are three scriptures where Jesus is teaching the disciples the importance of being proactive and not reactive in prayer life. Matthew's account explains why, "because the spirit is willing but the flesh is weak." As human beings, we find ourselves being reactive and not proactive. We watch what we eat after the clothes get tight or when the doctor tells us our health depends on it. We take the car to the mechanic when either the service engine soon light comes on or when it breaks down. We are almost always reactive and hardly ever proactive. Jesus instructs us to pray when the temptation surfaces, and once you ask him to keep you, then the Holy Spirit will empower you to resist the temptation. The spirit is definitely willing, but the flesh is indeed weak. However, Jude writes,

> Now to Him [God] who is able to keep you from stumbling, and present you faultless before the presence of His glory with exceeding great joy. Jude 1:24 (NKJV)

Both of the apostles Paul and Jude understood that we on our own are no match for the trickery of the enemy. But we serve a God who can enable us to overcome or even evade temptation. This is why God, immediately following Jesus's ascension, sent the Holy Spirit to assist us in overcoming the schemes of the enemy. Yes, we can control the urges of the flesh. We can be made whole and begin walking in shaloam. This is possible if we adhere to the Word of God and not our flesh. We are called to mortify or kill the deeds of the flesh, and we can do it by utilizing the Word of God, the presence of God, and the Spirit of God. God has sent the Holy Spirit to assist and preserve you.

> For this reason I also suffer these things; nevertheless I am not ashamed, for I know whom I have believed and am persuaded that He is able to keep what I have committed to Him until that Day. 2 Timothy 1:12 (NKJV)

> The Lord is your keeper; The Lord is your shade at your right hand. Psalm 121:5 (NKJV)

It is simple. He will keep if you commit. Just ask him now, "Dear Lord, I come to you now, asking you to help me mortify the deeds of my flesh. Keep me for evil, especially_____ [whatever sin you're struggling with]. You said if I confess my sin, you are faithful and just to forgive my sin and cleanse me from all unrighteousness. I believe your Word, and I receive my forgiveness and cleansing now in Jesus' name. Amen." Search yourself and begin to call out every sin you are struggling with, and the Lord will do the rest. God bless.

# Chapter 6

## The Ministry of the Holy Spirit

> Nevertheless I tell you the truth. It is to your advantage that I go away; for if I do not go away, the Helper will not come to you; but, if I depart, I will send Him to you. John 16:7 (NKJV)

This chapter is going to explain the ministry of the Holy Spirit and answer some of the age-old questions. Who is the Holy Spirit? What is his purpose or ministry? Why do we need him, and what's the importance of having him? I'd like to start by saying that the Holy Spirit is the third God of the Holy Trinity. He is the Spirit of God. He's not an it but a person. In the book of Genesis, it reads,

> In the beginning God created the heavens and the earth. And the earth was without form, and void; and darkness was upon the face of the deep and the *Spirit of God* was hovering over the face of the waters. Genesis 1:1–2 (NKJV)

The Hebrew word for God in this passage is Elohim, which is the plural name or God in the plural form. So when the wise guys approach you asking "Where is the word *trinity* in the Bible?" your response should be "It's not in there, however, God's plural name Elohim, which is used to describe the trinity, is approximately used in about 2,700 places in the Bible." God is a triune or tripartite God. In verse 26 of the first chapter of Genesis, God (Elohim) is speaking to himself about making man after themselves. Awesome! Let's read it.

> Let us make man in Our image, according to Our likeness; let them have dominion over the fish of the sea, over the birds of the air, and over the cattle, over all the earth and over every creeping thing that creeps on the earth. Genesis 1:26 (NKJV)

Other examples of God the Father manifesting in all three forms or components at once is found in the gospels.

> When He had been baptized, *Jesus* came up immediately from the water; and behold, the heavens were opened to Him, and He saw *the Spirit of God* descending like a dove and alighting upon Him. And suddenly a *voice came from heaven*, saying, "This is My beloved Son, in whom I am well pleased." Matthew 3:16–17 (NKJV)

> And John bore witness, saying, "I saw the Spirit descending from heaven like a dove, and He remained upon Him." John 1:32 (NKJV)

The Holy Spirit is the third part of the Godhead: God the Father, God the Son (Jesus), and God the Holy Spirit. The three make up one God, and they always work in concert with one another—God above man (the Father), God alongside man (Jesus), God inside of man (the Holy Spirit)—in those who would allow him in, that is. The Father established a covenant with Abraham. Jesus fulfilled and ratified the covenant, and the Holy Spirit effectuates the covenant. I could go on with a plethora of scripture to convince you, but let's move on. Jesus, before his death, burial, and glorious resurrection, stressed with urgency the necessity of his departure in order for the Holy Spirit to arrive.

> Nevertheless I tell you the truth. It to your advantage that I go away; for if I don't go away the Helper will not come to you; but if I depart, I will send Him to you. And when He has come, He will convict the world of sin, and of righteousness, and of judgment. John 16:7–8 (NKJV)

There is a three-part purpose why the Holy Spirit was sent, which also explains why we need him: (1) To convict the world of sin, (2) convict the world of righteousness, and (3) convict the world of judgment. Let's look at John 16:9-11(KJV):

Of sin, because they do not believe in Me; of righteousness, because I go to My Father and you see Me no more; of judgment, because the ruler of this world is judged.

His first purpose is to convict the world of sin. Unbelief is the foundation of sin and is the source of sinfulness that brings about eternal damnation. Jesus said, "No one comes to Him except the Father draws him." The Father uses the Holy Spirit to draws us unto salvation. Everyone who is born again is convicted and convinced by the Father through the Holy Spirit. There are many who, whether in church, home, work, prison, a bar, never expected or planned to be saved that day; however, the Father convicted and convinced them at that very moment to receive Jesus as Lord. Here are a few scriptures that line up with this passage.

Most assuredly, I say to you, he who hears My word and believes in Him who sent Me has everlasting life, and shall not come into judgment, but has passed from death into life. John 5:24 (NKJV)

Therefore I said to you that you will die in your sins; for if you do not believe that I am He, you will die in your sins. John 8:24 (NKJV)

So the Holy Spirit's first purpose is to introduce you to the gospel of Jesus Christ by convicting and convincing you that you and I need a savior, and that savior is Jesus Christ, the Son of the Living God.

The Holy Spirit's second purpose is to convict and convince (reprove) the world of righteousness. He does this by convicting and convincing us that our righteousness is *insufficient and useless.*

> But we are all like an unclean thing, And all our righteousness are like filthy rags; We all fade as a leaf, And our iniquities, like the wind, Have taken us away. Isaiah 64:6 (NKJV)

> For they being ignorant of God's righteousness, and seeking to establish their own righteousness, have not submitted to the righteousness of God. Romans 10:3 (NKJV)

We can do one of two things: we can either walk in Jesus's righteousness or walk in our own righteousness that we have established on our own. He convicts and convinces us that Jesus satisfied our righteous requirement and that by faith in him alone and his finished work on the cross can we be made righteous.

> But of Him you are in Christ Jesus, who became for us wisdom from God—and righteousness and sanctification and redemption. 1 Corinthians 1:30 (NKJV)

Even the righteousness of God, through faith in
Jesus Christ, to all and on all who believe. For there
is no difference; for all have sinned and fall short of
the glory of God, being justified freely by His grace
through the redemption that is in Christ Jesus,
whom God set forth as a propitiation by His blood,
through faith, to demonstrate His righteousness,
because in His forbearance God had passed over
the sins that were previously committed. Romans
3:22–25 (NKJV)

The third purpose of the Holy Spirit is to convict and convince
the world of judgment. To convince man that whoever believes
in Jesus Christ escapes eternal damnation and that everyone who
refuses to believe will be damned along with Satan.

He who believes in Him is not condemned; but
he who does not believe is condemned already,
because he has not believed in the name of the only
begotten Son of God. John 3:18 (NKJV)

Then He will also say to those on the left hand,
"Depart from Me, you cursed, into the everlasting
fire prepared for the devil and his angels." Matthew
25:41 (NKJV)

But the cowardly, unbelieving, abominable,
murderers, sexually immoral, sorcerers, idolaters,

and all liars shall have their part in the lake which
burns with fire and brimstone, which is the second
death. Revelation 21:8 (NKJV)

So let's recap, the Holy Spirit's primary job is to convict
and convince the world's populous of its sin. To convict and
convince us that without Jesus, we are eternally lost. Secondly,
to convict and convince us that our righteousness will *not* fulfill
the righteous requirement and we *must* receive and become the
righteousness of God through faith in Jesus Christ. And thirdly,
to convict and convince us to avoid eternal damnation, which is
the final judgment of Satan. That is so clear and concise. So easy
to understand.

One of the many names of the Holy Spirit is the Comforter.
The Greek word is *parakletos*, which means "counselor." Whenever
we are in doubt, confused, or need direction, the Holy Spirit will
impart God's divine providence. He is also referred to as the Spirit
of Truth. Another work he does in us is to reveal the truth in every
situation as it pertains to the Father's acceptable and perfect will
for your life. He (the Holy Spirit) is also your inner intercessor,
who prays on your behalf to both cleanse you and keep you in
purpose. If we would only train ourselves to listen to him and
allow him to do two things: (1) pray through you and (2) lead
you. How many times have you felt the urge to do something or
go somewhere and you didn't and later regretted not obeying the
urge and exclaiming, "Something told me!"? How about shouting
"Someone told me!"? The Holy Spirit is your built-in navigation

system. His assignment again is to lead you and keep you in God's divine providence or purpose. Allow him to do his job! One of my favorite passages of scripture, Romans 8:26-28 (NKJV), makes the Holy Spirit's mission clear and concise.

> Likewise the Spirit also helps in our weaknesses. For we do not know what we should pray for as we ought, but the Spirit Himself makes intercession for us with groanings which cannot be uttered.

> Now He who searches the hearts knows what the mind of the Spirit is, because He makes intercession for the saints according to the will of God. And we know that all things work together for good to those who love God, to those who are the called according to His purpose.

This passage fully explains just how the Holy Spirit operates or performs his purpose. He does it by being the inner intercessor, praying for our weaknesses, because he sees us from the inside out and can pray for us more effectively than we can for ourselves. It's like when we take a late-model vehicle to the mechanic and they don't troubleshoot like the mechanics did a decade or two ago; the mechanic plugs the vehicle into a computer in the shop. The computer in the vehicle syncs with the computer at the shop, and the computer gives a report to the mechanic of what is wrong with the vehicle. As a result, the mechanic repairs the vehicle. In like manner, the Holy Spirit searches our hard drive, which is our spirit, or heart, and intercedes to the Father, also convicting and convincing us to allow him to delete any malware or sin the enemy has installed in our life. Here is another passage of scripture that makes the point I am making crystal clear.

> For it is God which worketh in you both to will and
> to do of his good pleasure. Philippians 2:13 (KJV)

God has designed a foolproof system to aid us in our spiritual growth and maturity. God is actually residing on the inside of us in the form of the Holy Spirit. He can't get any closer to us than that. If we allow the Holy Spirit to do his job in us, we can and we will be made whole. We have not yet begun to tap into walking in and experiencing the benefits of shaloam! Don't you think it's about time? Allow the Holy Spirit to navigate you through this wicked and perverse world into an abundant life here on earth followed by eternal life in the presence of God our Heavenly Father, Jesus the Son, and the Holy Spirit of God and many others of believing brothers and sisters. Now that is a family reunion that will *never* end. Hallelujah!

# Chapter 7

## It's Time

It is time for the body of Christ to rise up to its full potential. It is not impossible to live a victorious Christian life at the level of perfection the Father requires. Religion has crippled many of us into believing that we can never live up to the expectations that the Father has for us, but it's to the contrary. If we begin to utilize the tools that were given us—his Word, his Son (Jesus), his Spirit, his angels, his exceedingly great and precious promises, etc.—then we see the reality of the Father giving us everything that pertains to life (*zoe*), the abundant life that Jesus promises in John 10:10, and godliness, God's ability through his Word, his Spirit, his presence, and Jesus's blood to keep us from falling and present us faultless before his glorious throne with exceeding great joy. We have lived an unbalanced life for too long when God has promised us a complete, whole, hale life. Shaloam! Let's look at a few scriptures.

> Beloved, I pray that you may prosper in all things
> and be in health, just as your soul prospers. 3 John
> 2 (NKJV)

There are three major areas we as believers are concerned about individually, and that is our health, our wealth, or being able to provide for ourselves and our loved ones, and what is most important of the three, our spiritual growth and maturity. The first two are the main areas in which the enemy attacks or manipulates in order to hinder or cripple us from the third, which is spiritual maturity and, inevitably, shaloam. Once again, there are other strategic and systematic areas of attack used by the enemy; however, these three are the most common.

> Now may the God of peace Himself sanctify you
> completely; and may your whole spirit, soul, and
> body be preserved blameless at the coming of our
> Lord Jesus Christ. He who calls you is faithful, who
> also will do it. 1 Thessalonians 5:23–24 (NKJV)

This benediction written by Apostle Paul expressed the Father's desire and purpose for us, his children. To sanctify or separate us completely, spirit, soul, and body, from the contaminants of the world and keep or preserve us that way until the return of Jesus Christ. He wants us to be whole, complete, walking in shaloam until the coming of Christ, and God the Father has given us all the tools we need to do so.

So to sum it all up, we must do the following: Realize that we are fearfully and wonderfully made by God. God sent his Son, Jesus, to redeem us, forgive and cleanse us, as well as intercede for us. The Father sent the Word to build our faith in him and his abilities, as well as to exercise our authority given to us by him to overcome every adverse attack of Satan, meanwhile, framing our world and thus walking in shloam (wholeness). God also sent the Holy Spirit to lead, comfort, convict, and convince us to enter, walk in, and even remain in the purpose that the Father has predestined for us, thus avoiding eternal damnation. We have all the tools to live a *zoe*, or abundant, life. In 2 Peter 1:3 (KJV), it reads,

> According as his divine power hath given unto us all things that pertain unto life and godliness, through the knowledge of him that hath called us to glory and virtue.

In other words, everything you will ever need to succeed has already been given. We have already been given access to all the tools to enjoy wholeness (shloam) and also live a godly life. It is my prayer that you rise up and use everything given you.

> For in Him dwells all the fullness of the Godhead bodily; and you are complete in Him, who is the head of all principality and power. Colossians 2:9–10 (NKJV)

Once again, the potentiality of becoming whole is mentioned in this passage, how to achieve completeness, wholeness, shaloam. Wholeness is a reality, and it can be your reality if you will walk according to the Word and yield yourself to the Lord's ordinances. You are complete in him! You are whole in him! You are victorious in him! You are fully equipped in him! Again, it is my prayer that you rise up and use everything given you by being one with him. Godpseed!

Printed in the United States
By Bookmasters